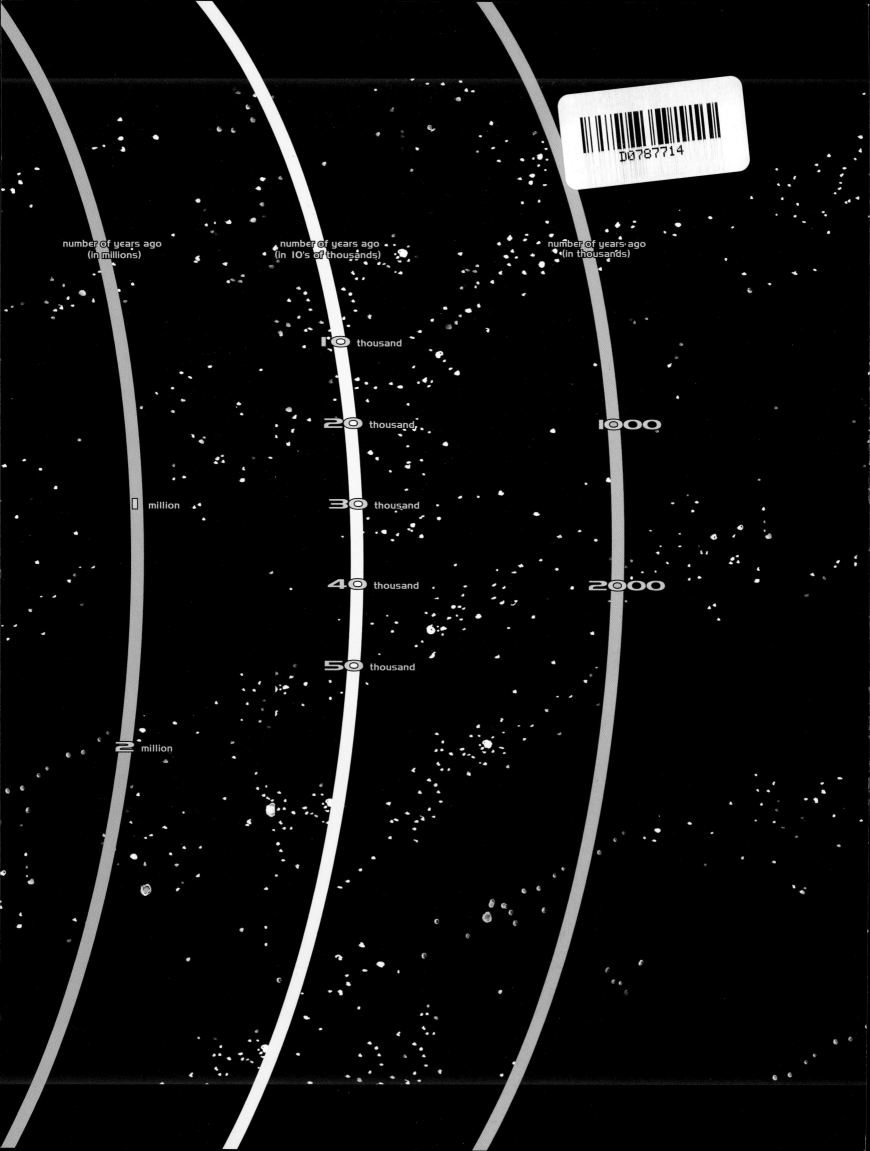

number of years ago
(in millions)

number of years ago
(in 10's of thousands)

number of years ago
(in thousands)

10 thousand

20 thousand

1000

30 thousand

40 thousand

2000

50 thousand

1 million

2 million

THE HORSE & THE IRON BALL

Lerner Publications

THE HORSE

& THE IRON BALL

A Journey through Time, Space, and Technology

Jerry Allan & Georgiana Allan

illustrated by Jerry Allan

Company • Minneapolis

Have you ever gazed at a fire?

Have you ever gazed at the sea?

Have you ever gazed at the stars in wonder...

for inspiration?

with questions?

Perhaps you have sensed
that is where we came from—

not symbolically,

not poetically,

but in fact.

This is the history of our beginnings,
dedicated to all those who wonder.

—Jerry Allan

Have you ever
wondered what
a horse
and an
iron ball have
in common?

Probably not,
but surprisingly...

they share a long
and interesting history.

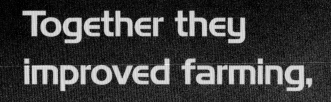

Together they improved farming,

and at times they became
the ultimate weapon.

For two millennia, horses provided

the major means of transportation...

until the 19th-century
invention of the iron horse.

Yes, in the world of sport and games,

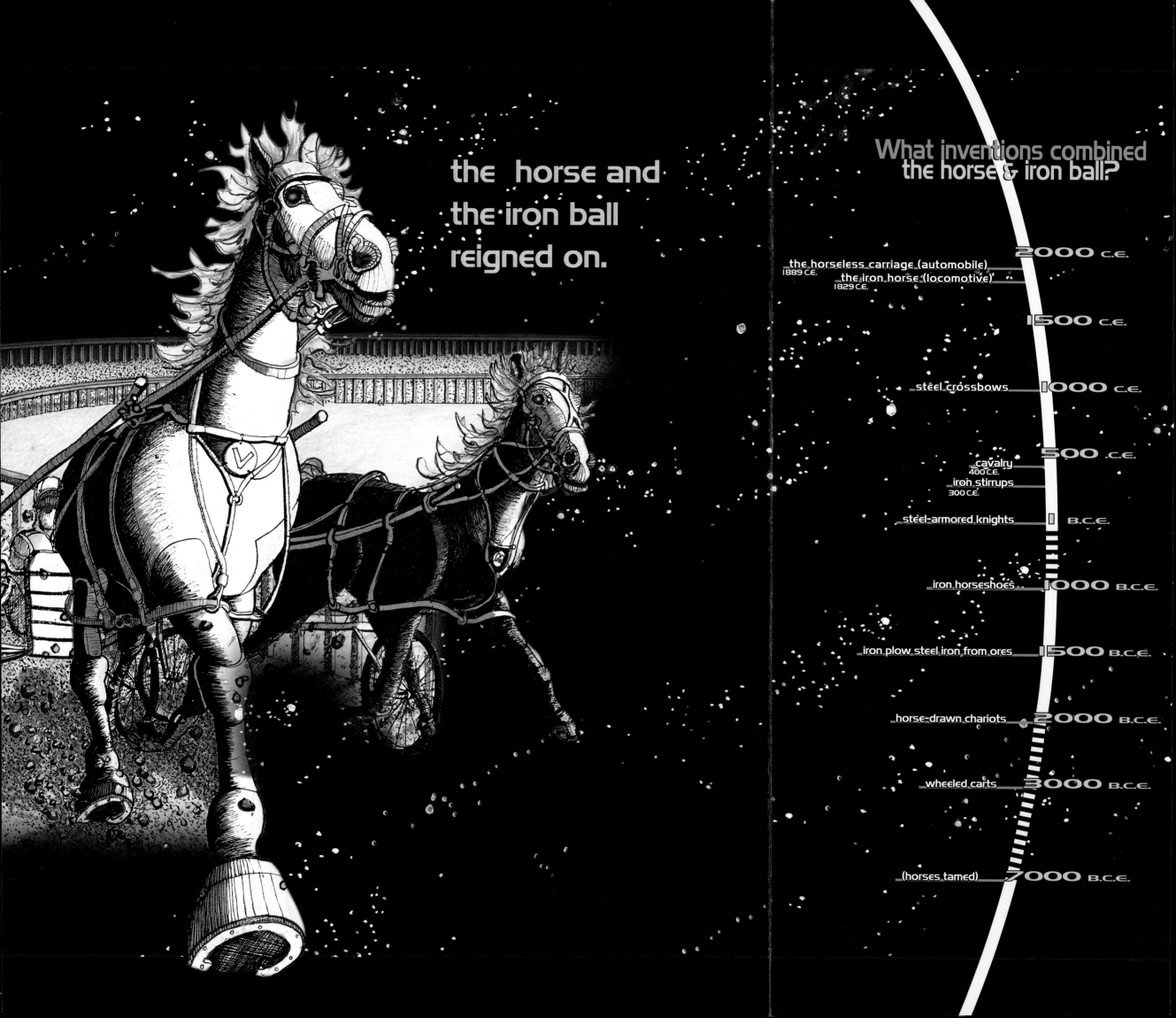

the horse and
the iron ball
reigned on.

What inventions combined
the horse & iron ball?

the horseless carriage (automobile)
1889 C.E.
the iron horse (locomotive)
1829 C.E.

2000 C.E.

1500 C.E.

steel crossbows — 1000 C.E.

500 C.E.

cavalry
400 C.E.
iron stirrups
300 C.E.

steel-armored knights — B.C.E.

iron horseshoes — 1000 B.C.E.

iron plow steel iron from ores — 1500 B.C.E.

horse-drawn chariots — 2000 B.C.E.

wheeled carts — 3000 B.C.E.

(horses tamed) — 7000 B.C.E.

Look back even further,
and you will see that it
was long, long ago
when their story began.

Q: With only hydrogen and helium, what can you make?

number of years ago

1 billion

2 billion

3 billion

4 billion

5 billion

6 billion

7 billion

ELEMENTS are the simplest form of a chemical. They are often noted by their abbreviations, such as H for hydrogen, He for helium, and Fe for iron.

8 billion

9 billion

10 billion

ATOMS are the building blocks of chemical elements.

11 billion

12 billion

first-generation stars, galaxies formed

13 billion   first atoms

big bang, universe begins

14 billion

15 billion

A: Only stars.

Twelve billion years ago, the universe was made up of large clouds of hydrogen and helium gases...

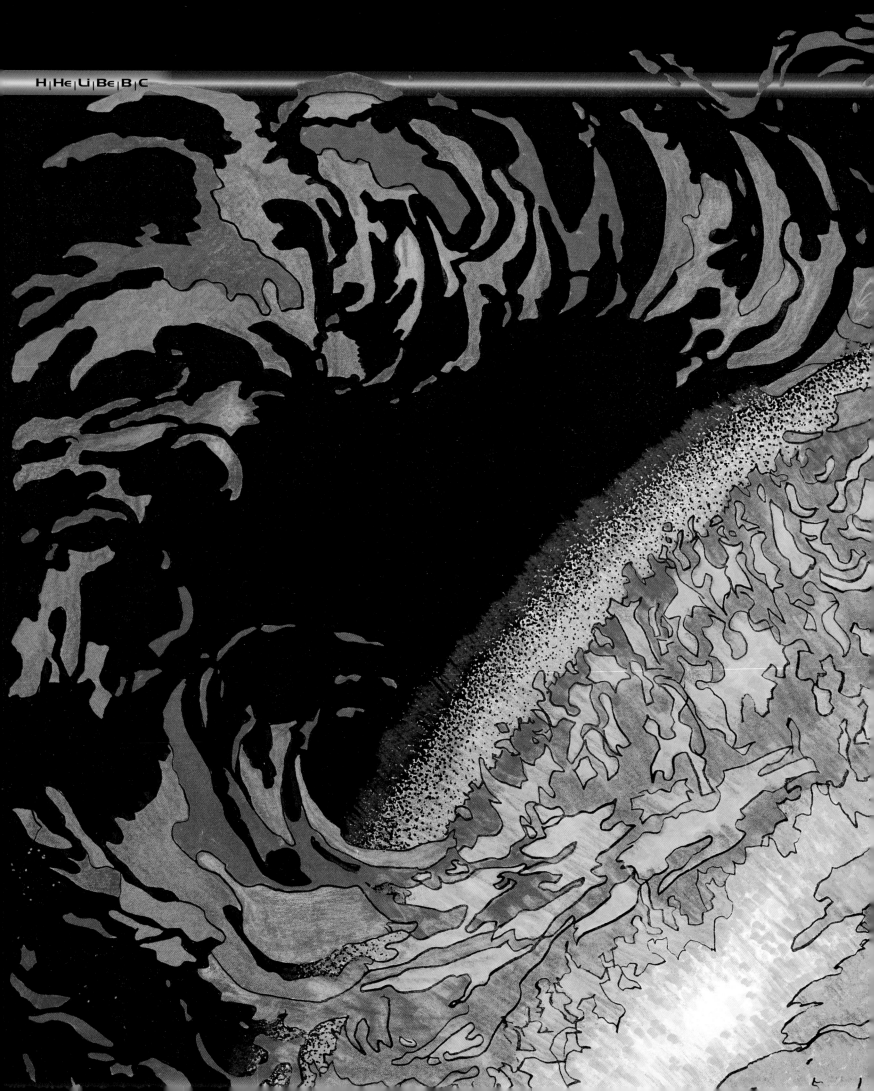

and some SUPER
STARS within newly
formed galaxies.
These stars became
the chemistry
factories for the
universe.

All stars, over their lifetime, fuse lighter elements into heavier ones.

But even super stars
only fuse the first
twenty-six elements,
up to iron (Fe).

When iron will not fuse...

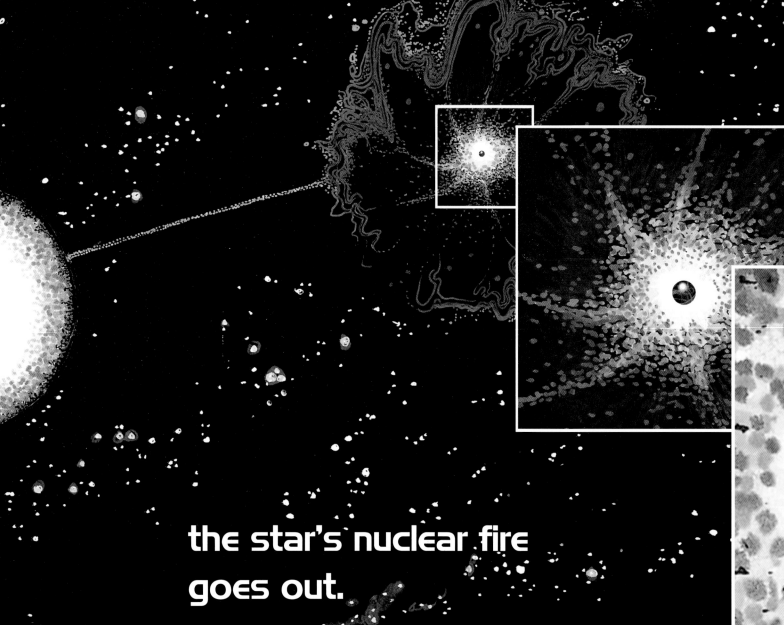

the star's nuclear fire
goes out.

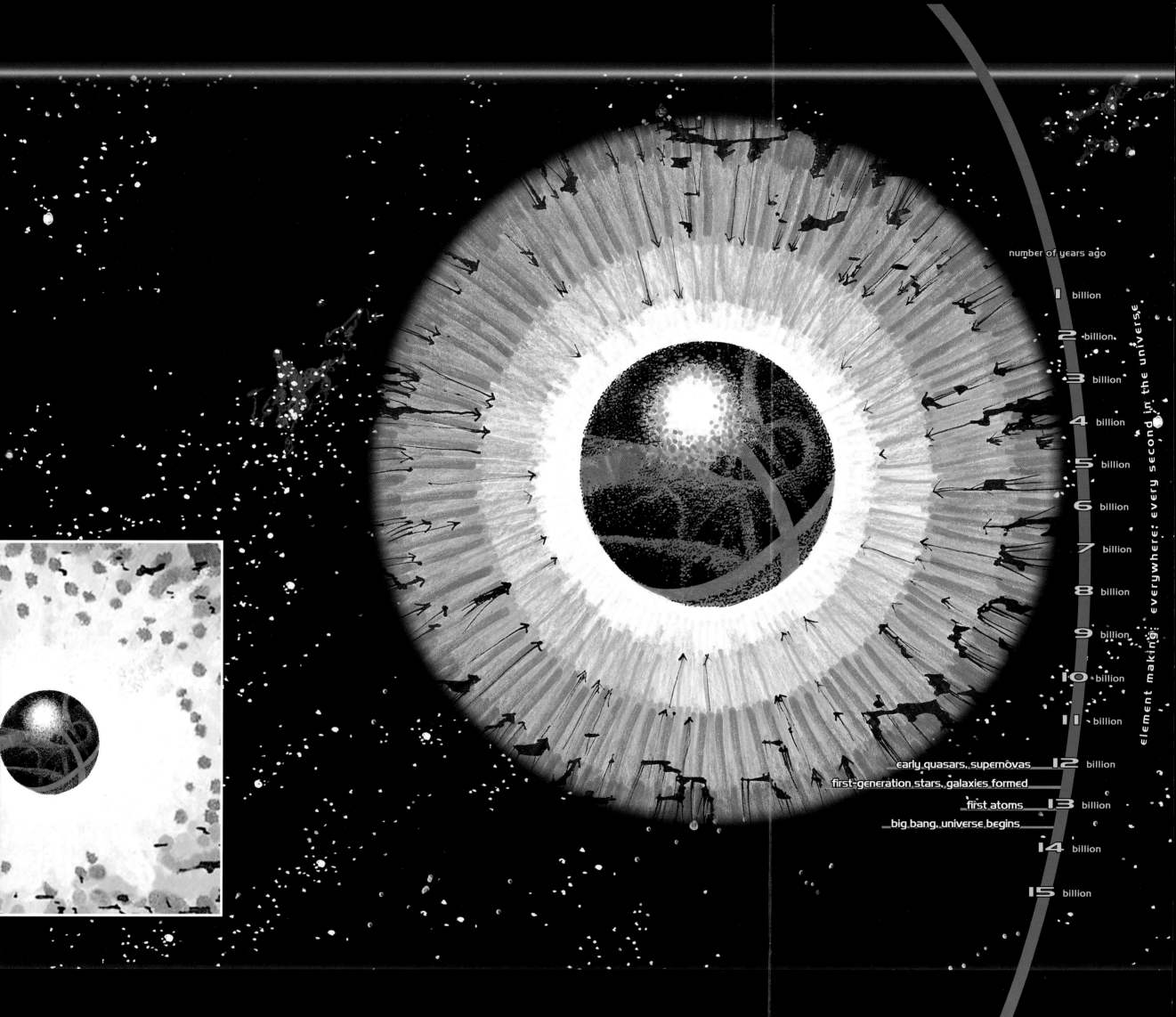

number of years ago

1 billion

2 billion

3 billion

4 billion

5 billion

6 billion

7 billion

8 billion

9 billion

10 billion

11 billion

early quasars, supernovas — 12 billion

first-generation stars, galaxies formed

first atoms — 13 billion

big bang, universe begins

14 billion

15 billion

element making: everywhere, every second in the universe.

Gravity takes over, and in a split second, the super star's iron core is crushed into a ball just a few miles wide.

The star's death is near.

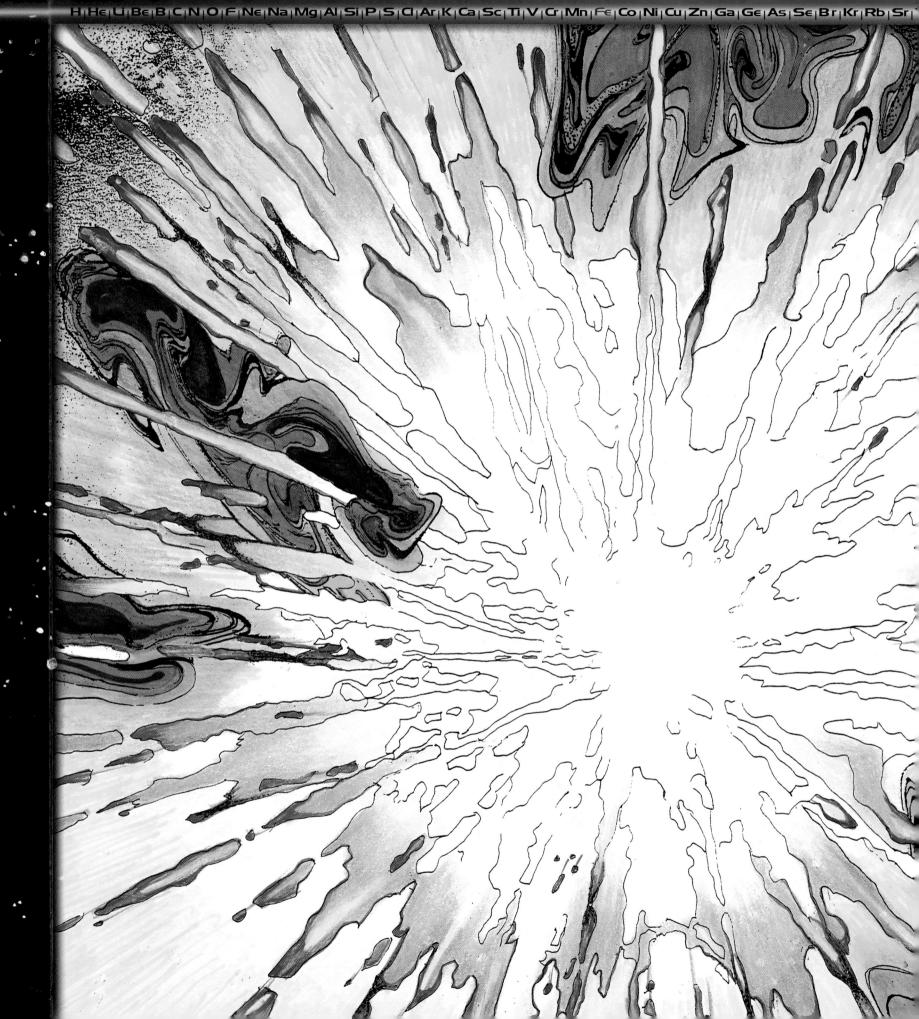

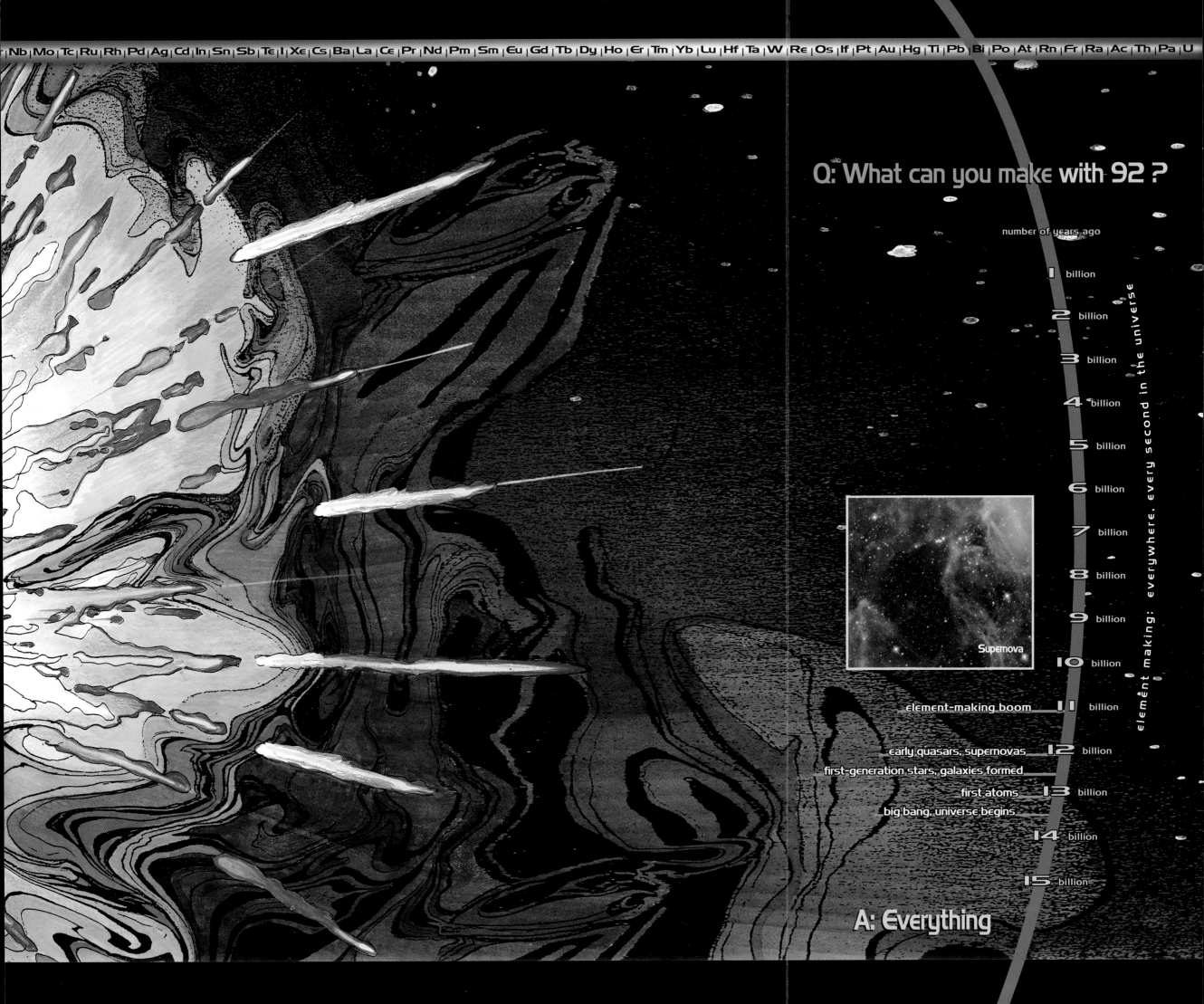

Q: What can you make with 92 ?

number of years ago

1 billion

2 billion

3 billion

4 billion

5 billion

6 billion

7 billion

8 billion

9 billion

Supernova

10 billion

element-making boom — 11 billion

early quasars, supernovas — 12 billion

first-generation stars, galaxies formed

first atoms — 13 billion

big bang, universe begins

14 billion

15 billion

A: Everything

element making: everywhere, every second in the universe

The iron ball suddenly rebounds, triggering an enormous supernova explosion. All the elements heavier than iron—including silver, gold, and uranium—are instantly created.

Remnants of the explosion surge through space. When the element-rich clouds of gases collide, matter clumps, forming protostars.

Long, long ago, in an arm of the Milky Way galaxy, one such collision caused a protostar to form.

Over millions of years of cooling, condensing, and collisions, protoplanets also formed. Meanwhile, the protostar grew. Its force of gravity pulled in more and more gases, until it finally ignited. This new star was our Sun.

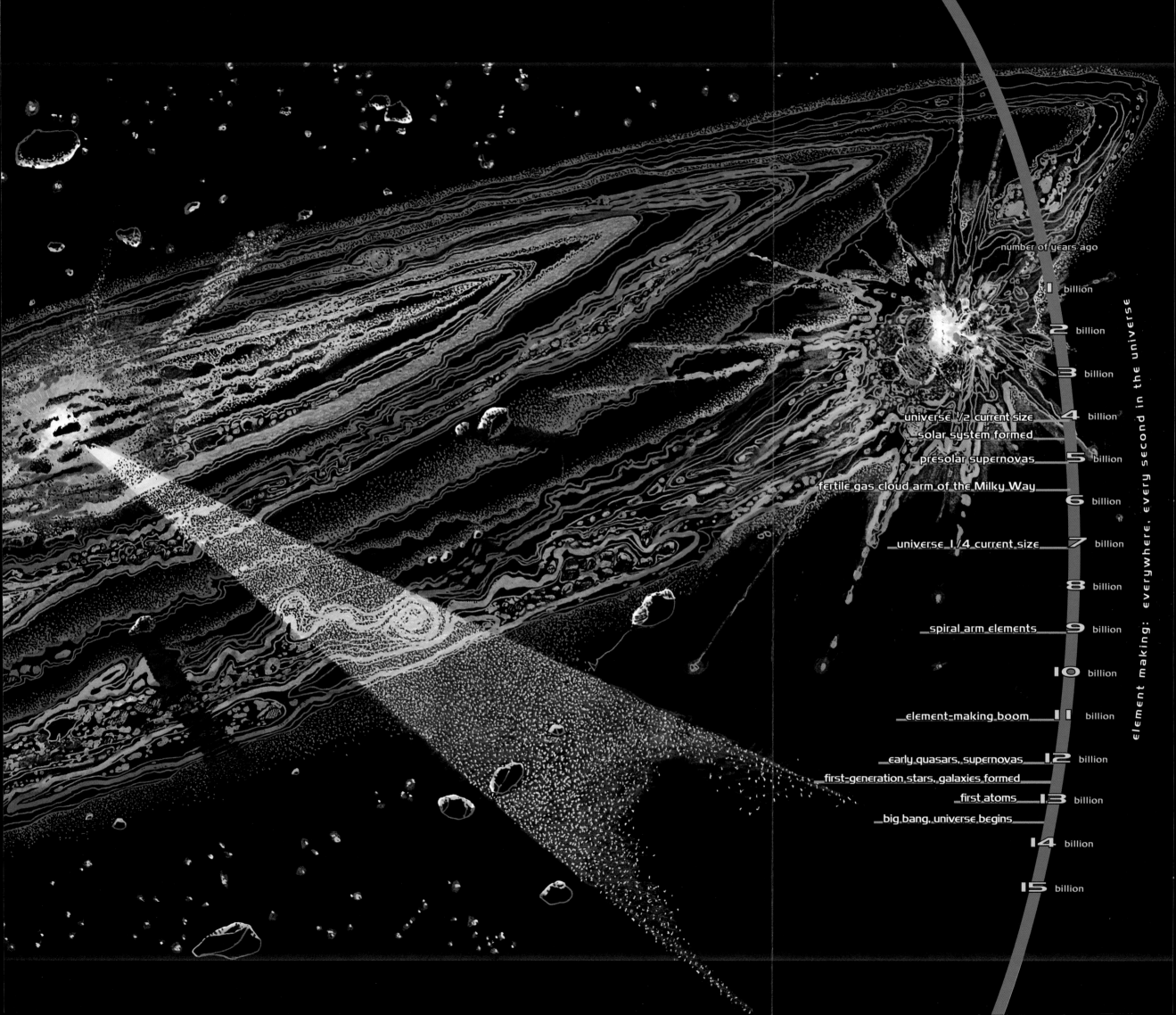

number of years ago

1 billion

2 billion

3 billion

4 billion — universe 1/2 current size

solar system formed
presolar supernovas — 5 billion

fertile gas cloud arm of the Milky Way — 6 billion

universe 1/4 current size — 7 billion

8 billion

spiral arm elements — 9 billion

10 billion

element-making boom — 11 billion

early quasars, supernovas — 12 billion

first-generation stars, galaxies formed
first atoms — 13 billion

big bang, universe begins

14 billion

15 billion

element making: everywhere, every second in the universe

Its solar winds swept away the remaining dust and gases, revealing a group of nine orbiting planets.

One planet was just the right distance from the Sun for water to remain liquid. That planet was Earth.

As the Earth's crust cooled, molten rock churned below, cracking the surface.

Volcanoes erupted through the cracks, spewing minerals and gases, and forming land and an atmosphere around the planet.

Meteorites and comets
bombarded the surface with
more minerals and ice.

Rain formed,
and water pooled
in craters.

early life (blue-green algae)

first life on Earth

number of years ago 4 billion 3 billion

Lightning energized the atmosphere. The pools heated and cooled. Chemicals combined randomly and eventually formed organic compounds that became life.

Life evolved—from simple cells to more complex plants and animals—and eventually moved from sea to land.

Reptiles, dinosaurs, and mammals evolved.

first blue-green algae

first seaweed-like plants

soft animals animals (sponges and worms)

first invertebrates

jawless fishes

amphibians and trees

reptiles

winged insects

Ice ages

coal (fuel for iron horses)

first frogs

first dinosaurs; flowers

giant dinosaurs; winged reptiles

early mammals

Brachiosaurs

first birds

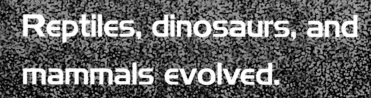

billion | I billion | 600 million | 500 million | 400 million | 300 million | 200 million

Eohippus (early horse) fossil

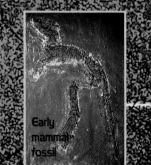

Early mammal fossil

One of these mammals was the ancestor of the horse.

So...

What do a horse and an

Petroleum or oil (fuel for "horseless carriage")

dinosaur extinction

first primates; modern carnivores

early horse

early cats; dogs; & monkeys;

iron ball have in common?

early whales

first grass (fuel for horses)
modern mammals

first ape-like humans

elephants

30 million   20 million   10 million

As you can see,
without the iron
ball, there would
never have been
the horse.

You too are a superstar.

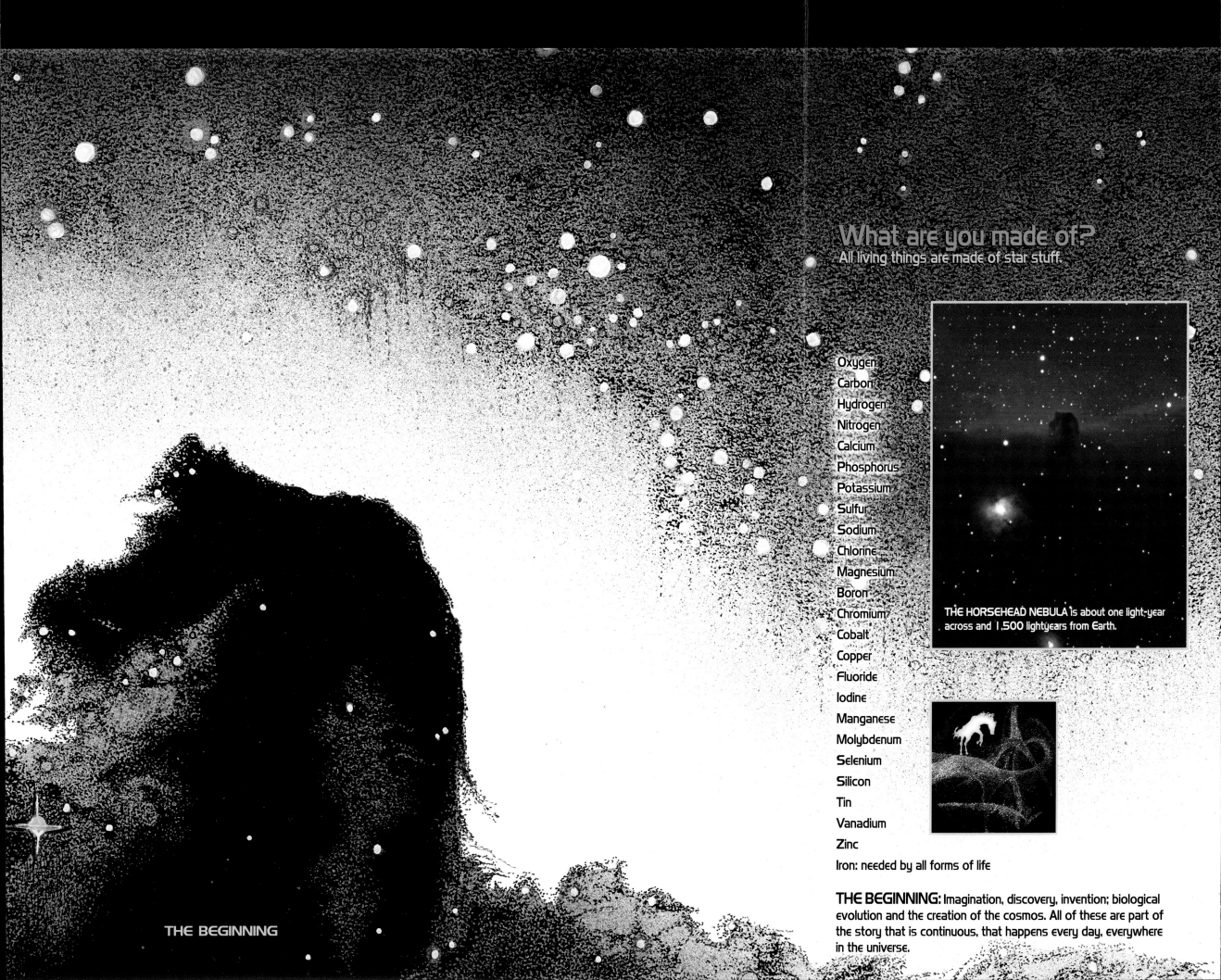

What are you made of?

All living things are made of star stuff.

Oxygen
Carbon
Hydrogen
Nitrogen
Calcium
Phosphorus
Potassium
Sulfur
Sodium
Chlorine
Magnesium
Boron
Chromium
Cobalt
Copper
Fluoride
Iodine
Manganese
Molybdenum
Selenium
Silicon
Tin
Vanadium
Zinc
Iron: needed by all forms of life

THE HORSEHEAD NEBULA is about one light-year across and 1,500 lightyears from Earth.

THE BEGINNING: Imagination, discovery, invention; biological evolution and the creation of the cosmos. All of these are part of the story that is continuous, that happens every day, everywhere in the universe.

THE BEGINNING

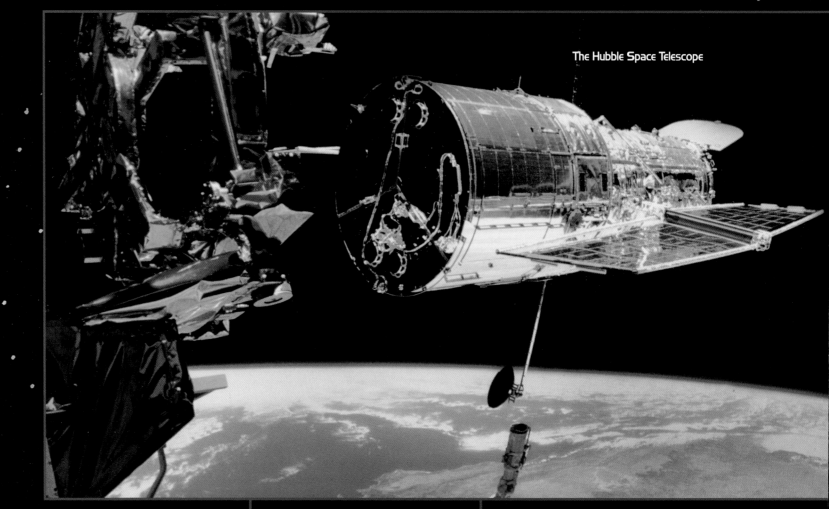

The Hubble Space Telescope

pages 8-19

Iron is one of the most common chemical substances found in the Earth's crust, but it is never found there in its pure form. Almost all iron occurs in ores (mineral or rock deposits).

Steel is produced by refining (purifying) iron and mixing it with other metals, including carbon and usually manganese.

The **Iron Age** is period of time that began in about 1,000 B.C.E., when the working of iron became widespread. When iron was combined with the horse, the technology of agriculture, warfare, and transportation changed dramatically.

Blacksmiths are craftsmen in the art of ironworking (pounding hot iron into shape).

Blacksmiths pounded hot iron into curved shapes to make **horseshoes,** which are nailed to a horse's hooves. When horses were used for riding and working on uneven ground, their hooves would wear down, causing pain and injury. Horseshoes transformed the horse into a durable beast of burden.

pages 20-21

Elements are the simplest form of a chemical; they are the basic substances that make up everything we know, from stars to stones to bones. Elements are often noted by their abbreviations, such as H for hydrogen, He for helium, and Fe for iron. There are 92 natural elements.

Hydrogen is the most basic and lightest of all elements. Hydrogen makes up 75% of the known mass of the universe.

Atoms are the building blocks of chemical elements. Atoms are so tiny that the smallest speck of matter that can be seen with an ordinary microscope contains more than 10 billion atoms. Every atom is made up of even smaller particles called protons, neutrons, and electrons.

The **big bang theory** is a widely accepted theory that the universe was created from an immensely hot, dense point that exploded 12 to 15 billion years ago. The theory is based on the fact that all galaxies are speeding away from one another; therefore, at the very beginning of the universe, everything must have been together.

The **early universe** came to be after the big bang explosion cooled. This cooling allowed the simplest atoms to form into large clouds of gas. Over the next billion years, the gases clumped together to form the first generation of stars.

pages 22-23
A **star** is a sphere of gas that produces light as it generates energy through nuclear fusion. The simplest element, hydrogen, is

Low-mass stars are stars that convert hydrogen to helium, then helium to carbon, before they swell and die. Our Sun is a low-mass star.

High-mass stars (super stars), with their larger gravitational force, fuse elements up to silicon (Si).

pages 24-29
The Life Cycle of a Star
During their lifetime, all stars must battle the force responsible for their creation—gravity. Gravity draws together gas and dust, eventually causing the star to ignite. As gravity pulls inward,

The Eagle nebula

enabling the next heavier elements to serve as the star's fuel.

Depending upon a star's makeup and mass, it may live for 1 billion to 100 billion years.

The Death of a Super Star
A star does not have enough energy to fuse iron, and its nuclear fire goes out. Gravity takes over, and the massive, unsupported weight of the star's outer layers comes crashing in on the star's planet-sized iron core, crushing it into an iron ball only a few miles wide. Iron, nature's most stable element, rebounds, creating a shock wave which triggers a supernova.

A **supernova** is a colossal explosion that blows a star to pieces. Within an instant of a supernova, the remaining 66 elements heavier than iron are created. The explosion rockets the tenth the speed of light (equal to traveling from the Sun to the orbit of Uranus in one day). Supernova shock waves are thought to be the primary initiators of new star formation.

Protostars are stars that are in the process of forming.

Our own galaxy, called the **Milky Way,** consists of about 100 million stars.

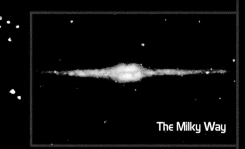

The Milky Way

pages 32-33
A **planet** is a large rocky, gaseous, or icy body that is in orbit around a star.

Protoplanets are planets that are in the process of forming.

pages 34-35
A solar system is all the planets, asteroids, comets, and dust that orbit a sun. Our solar system was formed about 5 billion years ago. It includes the Sun, nine planets, and their moons.

The **Eco-Zone** is an area a certain distance from the Sun where water can exist naturally in a liquid state (between 0° and 100° C). Closer to the sun, water vaporizes; farther away it freezes.

pages 36-37
The gases that surround a planet are called its **atmosphere.** Volcanoes belched up steam and gases mixed with frozen ice and

vapors from bombarding comets to form the Earth's early atmosphere. Earth's atmosphere is composed mostly of nitrogen and oxygen.

During the 100 million years the Earth was forming, numerous collisions and the decay of radioactive elements heated the young planet. Heat caused heavier matter to sink to the center, forming a super-dense iron ball about 2,000 kilometers across. The Earth's solid **iron core** created a strong gravitational force to hold on to its newly formed atmosphere. The iron core also created a large magnetic field that shielded the planet from harmful radiation. Molten materials surrounding the iron core produced Earth's active, ever-renewing geology.

A **meteor** is a solid object from space that passes through the atmosphere of a planet or moon.

A **comet** is a bright body that is made up of frozen gases, ice, and dust particles.

pages 38-39
Bacteria are the simplest organisms, made up of only one cell, that are among the smallest of all living things. The first living things on Earth were probably bacteria.

Stromatolites are living rocklike humps composed of layers of slimy bacteria and bits of sand. For more than a billion years, stromatolites were the only living things on Earth.

pages 40-41
A **fossil** is the remains or traces of a plant or animal that lived long ago, preserved in the Earth's crust. Much of what we know about the evolution of life was learned by studying

fossils. The Earth's oldest fossil, containing evidence of bacterial life, is 3.86 billion years old.

The **Hubble Space Telescope** is a large telescope that orbits the Earth outside its atmosphere (about 380 miles above the surface) to gather clear images of objects in space. It was launched from a space shuttle in 1990. The Hubble telescope is named for astronomer Edwin Hubble (1889-1953), who made important discoveries about galaxies that helped explain the size, structure, and evolution of the universe.

pages 42-43
A **nebula** is a region in space where large clouds of dust, gas, and remnants of supernovas are visible because of reflected or absorbed starlight. Nebulas are the nurseries for the birth of new stars.

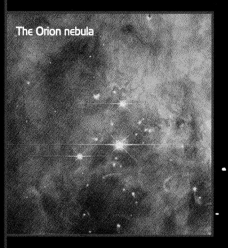

The Orion nebula

A **light-year** is the distance that light travels in one year, equaling 5.87 trillion (5.87 thousand billion) miles.

Superstar: A person who is widely acclaimed for exceptional accomplishments or abilities.

SELECTED BIBLIOGRAPHY

Attenborough, David. *Life on Earth: A Natural History.* Boston: Little, Brown and Company, 1979.

Beiser, Arthur. *The Earth.* New York: Time-Life Books, 1971.

Calder, Nigel. *Timescale: An Atlas of the Fourth Dimension.* New York: Viking, 1983.

Clark, Stuart. *Universe in Focus: The Story of the Hubble Telescope.* New York: Barnes & Noble Books, 1997.

Gallant, Roy A. *National Geographic Picture Atlas of Our Universe.* Washington, D.C., National Geographic Society, 1994.

Gore, Rick. "Expanding Worlds: The Dawn of Humans," National Geographic Magazine 191, no. 5 (May 1997).

Isenbart, Hans-Heinrich. *The Kingdom of the Horse.* Frankfurt, Germany: C. J. Bucher, 1969.

Kirshner, Robert P. and Roger H. Ressmeyer. "Supernova: Death of a Star," National Geographic Magazine 173, no. 5 (May 1988).

Lapp, Ralph E. *Matter.* New York: Time-Life Books, 1974.

Monastersky, Richard. "The Rise of Life on Earth," National Geographic Magazine 193, no. 3 (March 1998).

Newcott, William R. "Time Exposures: The Hubble Telescope Views the Universe from Space," National Geographic Magazine 191, no. 4 (April 1997).

Reston, James Jr. "Orion: Where Stars Are Born," National Geographic Magazine 188, no. 6 (December 1995).

Sagan, Carl, *Cosmos.* New York: Random House, 1985.

Scientific American. *Cosmology + 1: Readings from Scientific American,* with an Introduction by Owen Gingerich.. San Francisco: W. H. Freeman and Company, 1977.

Smithsonian Institution, *Fire of Life: The Smithsonian Book of the Sun.* Washington, D.C.: Smithsonian Exposition Books; New York: Distributed by Norton, 1981.

Thuan, Trinh Xuan. *The Birth of the Universe: The Big Bang and After.* New York: H.N. Abrams, 1993.

Time-Life Books. *The Cosmos: Voyage through the Universe.* Alexandria, Virginia, 1989.

ABOUT THE AUTHORS

JERRY ALLAN is the founder and president of Criteria Architects, a design firm that coordinates architects, landscape architects, graphic designers, biochemists, physicists, sculptors, painters, and photographers. Jerry is also a professor at the Minneapolis College of Art and Design. **GEORGIANA ALLAN** is a designer and writer, wife and mother. Jerry and Georgiana work together on an array of projects that include product design, creativity training, leadership training, and meeting facilitation. They teach creativity to all kinds of people, from children to corporate executives, and frequently lecture and write on their favorite subject. The Allans live in Afton, Minnesota.

PHOTO ACKNOWLEDGMENTS: Photographs are reproduced courtesy of: NASA, pp. 27, 45, 46, Lunar and Planetary Institute, p. 33, © Robert Calentine/Visuals Unlimited, p. 39, American Museum of Natural History, p. 41 (top), © Daniel Heuclin/Natural History Photographic Agency, p. 41 (bottom), © John Gleason/Celestial Images, p. 43.

Back cover photos: © Albert J. Copley/Visuals Unlimited (top); NASA (lower left and right).

Lerner Publications Company
241 First Avenue North
Minneapolis, MN 55401 U.S.A.

website address: www. lernerbooks.com

Library of Congress Cataloging-in-Publication Data

Allan, Jerry, 1943-
        The horse & the iron ball: a journey through time, space, and technology / Jerry Allan and Georgiana Allan ; illustrated by Jerry Allan.
        p.   cm.
Includes bibliographical references.
Summary: A pictorial history of the universe that explains how all things are related—even a horse and an iron ball.
        ISBN 0-8225-2158-X (lib. bdg. ; alk. paper)
Cosmology—Juvenile literature. [1. Cosmology. 2. Universe.] I. Title: Horse and the iron ball. II. Allan, Georgiana. III. Title.
        QB893 .A45 2000
523.1—dc21   00-008139

Printed and bound in Thailand

1 2 3 4 5 6 05 04 03 02 01 00

cosmic time

biological time

number of years ago
(in billions)

number of years ago
(in 100's of millions)

vertebrate animals

elephants

1 billion   soft animals (sponges and worms)

first ape-like humans

first seaweed-like plants

first grass (fuel for horses); modern mammals

first blue-green algae

early whales

2 billion   oxygen replaces CO2 atmosphere

early cats, dogs, & monkeys

shallow seas

early horse

2/3 of Earth's land formed

first primates; modern carnivores

3 billion   first continents

dinosaur extinction

living reefs on Earth (bacterial stromatolites)

petroleum, or oil (fuel for "horseless carriage")

photosynthesis

4 billion   universe 1/2 current size; first life on earth

100 million

solar system formed; Earth formed

early mammals

5 billion   presolar supernovas

fertile gas cloud arm of the Milky Way

first birds

6 billion

Brachiosaurs

7 billion   universe 1/4 current size

200 million

8 billion

giant dinosaurs; winged reptiles

9 billion   spiral arm elements

first dinosaurs; flowers

first frogs

10 billion

coal (fuel for iron horses)

11 billion   element-making boom

300 million   Ice ages

12 billion   early quasars, supernovas

birds

first-generation stars, galaxies formed

reptiles

13 billion   first atoms

winged insects

big bang; universe begins

amphibians and trees

14 billion

15 billion

400 million